Publisher:
Bruno Alfieri
Technical consultant:
Walter Beltrami
Editors:
Ippolito Alfieri, Silvia Giacobone
Photos:
Roberto Carrer, Gabriela Noris, Guy Mangiamele
Graphic design:
Giordano Barazzetti
Production:
Massimo Fabbri, Attilio Chiozza
Translation:
Jane Glover

INDEX

5 Foreword
7 Design
31 Life on board
41 Mechanics and safety
65 Driving impressions

ISBN 88-85880-55-X CL 41-0242-8

La Collection®

Società per la Storia e l'Immagine dell'Automobile
I-20125 Milano, via Ponte Seveso 25

PRINTED AND BOUND IN ITALY
by Grafiche Editoriali Padane, Cremona, March 1992.

MERCEDES-BENZ

SL

300 - 300.24 - 500 - 600

Bruno Alfieri
Road Test: Giancarlo Baghetti

AUTOMOBILIA

S SL 500

FOREWORD

The overwhelming sensation for anyone owning an SL can be summed up in one word: pride. A noble sentiment experienced by anyone who loves an object because they admire it. They like it because it is beautiful but also, and above all, because they know its qualities, most of which are hidden. Externally there is only the physical and formal aspect of design that is self-critical and aware of its own value. An SL will never be a *voyante* car. First impressions are not particularly striking, then one notices its lines and shape and next the brain takes in its real identity: finally comes admiration. Unlike some café roadsters from the Fifties – attractive, noisy, super-fast and fragile – an SL is a car that has been thought out in every mechanical and formal detail. The suspensions and engine are exactly what they should be. The bodywork, result of careful and extensive research, is not designed intuitively but contains a distillation of aristocracy in its every curve, line and protuberance. For this and other resasons, I shall try to use the following pages to show that anyone who drives an SL knows perfectly well that he is the luckiest, and proudest, of mortals.

Two Mercedes-Benz in coupé (with the hard-top) and roadster versions.

At Mercedes-Benz, car design is not a matter of pure chance. Taking a look at the 35-year-old history of the SL is only one way of rendering proof to this. The different SL generations with their characteristic design elements have always set the course for successive models as well as other car makes. There are manifold reasons for this.

Mercedes-Benz has always followed the principle that an eye-catching car design must not be the end in itself. Experience has shown that a car design which stands out against others by means of fancy avant-garde form elements is bound to be outdated quicker than those cars which deliberately shun such effects. It is a matter of fact that every shape undergoes an ageing process until is no longer fashionable. But this ageing process can be speeded up artificially as a means to increase the demand by introducing a new design and hence consciously inducing a product ageing process.

Mercedes-Benz has traditionally gone in the opposite direction. Particularly with the SL design. The long model cycles prove this. And it is especially this longevity of the SL series the designers have to take as a yardstick. The SL with the internal designation R 107, for example, which is now being succeeded by the R 129, has hardly lost any of its attraction since it first came out. This is an inestimable compliment – and a great challenge – for the Mercedes designers.

The following table illustrates that every SL generation has been trend-setting in design with its innovative power since the SL legend began in the mid-Fifties. A Mercedes-Benz, this can be said today, always sets the course and in every case sets an example. Following are some corner-stones in the history of innovative SL design: 1954: gull-wing doors on the first 300 SL for improved access; aerodynamic wheel arch panel on the 300 SL; long bonnet scoops on the 300 SL for a low front section and greater rigidity; pully retracted pull-lever door handles on the 300 SL.

The three profiles of the SL revealed in Bruno Sacco's photomontage. Which is the prettiest?

The Mercedes-Benz 300 SL Roadster with a 6-cylinder 2996 cc engine (1957-1963), the open version and heir of the famous 300 SL sports coupé with gull-wing doors. 554 were built. This bird's eye-view photograph highlights the two relief mouldings along the bonnet and the distinctive shape of the Mercedes-Benz sports-car radiator.

1957: stylistically integrated headlamp unit with indicators, highbeams and fog lights on the 300 SL convertible; fully retractable soft top with cover flap and separate hard top; 1963: pagoda-shaped coupé roof for achieving entry and access conditions similar to those in a saloon despite the low overall height of the 230 SL; low bodywork height due to wide-track chassis on the 230 SL conveying the impression of light weight; 1971: wrap-round indicator lamps for high perceptual safety on the 350 SL; ribbed rear lamps for dirt deflection on the 350 SL; fully padded safety steering wheel with large-surface hoot pad on the 350 SL; lateral impact protection strips at bumper level with integrated rubber profiles on the 350 SL; dirt-deflection system consisting of special-shape strips on the A-pillars and around the rear windscreen on the 350 SL for better visibility front and rear; 1989: models 300 SL/500 SL: new bumper design with invisible energy-absorbing elements in combination with even-surfaced lateral and door sill panels of glass-fibre reinforced plastic in a metallic shade. For the first time the bodywork is free of oddly projecting protective parts making for higher functionality and greater ease of repairs; new windscreen pillar design with multi-functional outer frame in the colour of the car as linking element flush with the outer skin between bonnet, front fender, door and roof on the 300 SL/500 SL; newly-designed interior appointments for even greater comfort on the 300 SL/500 SL; SL face harmoniously integrated in the front bumper and bonnet section and almost flush with the outer skin, with optimized aerodynamic grille of anodized aluminium louvres in titanium anthracite on the 300 SL/500 SL.

General features

We try to resume the basic features of SL and Mercedes-Benz design. The new SL has its first public appearance at the 1989 Geneva Motor Show. And self-assuredly it bears the modern features of a legend the beginnings of which date back 35 years. This SL image is above all the merit of the Mercedes-Benz designers, who today, after many years of creative work on the new Mercedes convertible, frankly admit: "This was the most difficult and most challenging task we ever faced".

The team of chief designer Bruno Sacco has succeeded, however, not only to establish the link between the new SL and its distinctive predecessor model, successfully marketed since 1971, but also to consistently pursue the ideals of the legendary first 300 SL of the 50s.

The design is trailblazing – just like all its predecessors, which have not lost any of their appeal and it is geared towards the future, anticipating the pace of time. Exotic

The Mercedes-Benz 350 SL (1971-1980), driven by the powerful V8 3499 cc engine. Skilful design work smoothed out all the masses giving it the look of a technologically perfect and authoritative product. The front end has been straightened, in this later model, and the light clusters are horizontal.

This design is still a long way from the SL's definitive lines. The cut of the rear part is futuristic but is too much of a departure from the Mercedes-Benz style.

This is the coupé version of the SL seen in the previous design, with slight modifications. The line of the roof is original but has too much of an American look about it.

fancies of shape, condemned to be short-lived, are not in line with this philosophy. Concessions in this respect would have meant to sacrifice the marque identity and the SL image.

The uniqueness of an SL is emphasized by some distinctive design characteristics: the extended bonnet with the SL radiator grille, an aesthetically appealing entity achieved through the perfect symbiosis of shape and function, the squat roof as well as the compact rear section. On the basis of these design features, the newcomer, too, will occupy its place in the row of the "typical SL models".

There is hardly a greater compliment for the Mercedes-Benz designers. For "typical SL" also stands for classic elegance, for dynamics and power. The reasons for the fact that the new SL suggests such concepts as tradition, high value, prestige, safety, comfort and performance by its mere outer shape are to be found in a complex and subtle design process.

The greatest difficulty the Mercedes-Benz designers faced besides creating a typical SL concept with stylistic attractiveness reaching beyond the turn of the millennium, was that they had to reconcile the two appearances of the new SL: with the soft top fully retracted and with the roof (soft or hard top) in position.

This aim of the total stylistic harmonization of all appearances has been achieved. This has not least been possible due to the development of numerous innovative design features such as the sensor-controlled roll-over bar and an integral belt and seat design.

This styling forms a perfect unity with technology. All the more precious appears the dynamic, powerful yet not forced flow of lines of the new SL series. This is achieved by the following design measures: extended bonnet reaching low down to the front; short and compact-shaped roof; rear with compact yet flowing lines; even-surfaced sides with an aerodynamically streamlined wedge shape; roof construction forming an aesthetic entity with the bodywork; organically embedded windscreen; inclined A-pillar gently moving up from the front fender with new dirt-deflecting system; sportly shaped flared wheel arches; refined appealingly shaped and newly dimensioned SL radiator grille with anodized aluminium louvres in titanium anthracite; in shape and function logically integrated head and rear lamps.

The exterior design is complemented by a generous interior, adding to the powerful appeal of the bodywork, which is characterized by: a safety standard unique for a convertible; great stability; hitherto unattained functionality and ergonomy; extraordinary comfort standards; a sound dose of sportiness.

All these individual measures together with an appealing overall shape and top-class engineering come to form a perfect entity: the new SL. This new SL furnishes further proof of the leading role Mercedes-Benz design plays in the automotive world. There are certain styling principles underlying the work of the Mercedes-Benz designers. Some of them are: 1. With the increasing similarity of technical and stylistic features, the symbol value and character of a car are characteristics gaining increasing importance. Mercedes cars emit signals which are unique in their classic appeal. 2. There is a permanent solution neither to style nor to technology. This is why for the designers automobile styling is a continuous innovative process aiming at increasing the aesthetic experience. 3. Mercedes-Benz design is a reflection of its quality. Technical functions and traditional values meet in an aesthetic shape to form a convincing symbiosis.

It was only in this way that the new SL was able to become not the stylistic fashionable end in itself but the characterful new SL. Powerful in its appearance yet with amazingly compact dimensions. Although the new-generation SL opens up new design dimensions, it remains true to the design philosophy characteristic of Mercedes-Benz: it is as close to the SL introduced in 1971 (vertical product homogeneity) as to

With this design there is an approach to the definitive version. The rear wheels are faired, a stylistic tendency which was much in vogue in the Thirties.

A full-size epowood model. This is part of the continuing research into the project's shape, although before building the lifesize model around twenty models had been built in 1:5 scale.

all contemporary models (horizontal product homogeneity).

From the first sketch to a masterpiece

"At the beginning there was the challenge. At the end there was the SL fascination". With these words Mercedes-Benz designers describe what they feel today, at the launch of the new SL. It is true that never before the team of chief designer Bruno Sacco had to face such a great challenge.

This is nothing out of the ordinary as a Mercedes-Benz sports car more than any other car builds up a field of tension: dynamic sportiness on the one hand and unobtrusive elegance on the other have to coalesce to form a stylistic entity.

Additionally, the model history going back 35 years constitutes a unique frame. Moulding a new car as the emotionally consistent continuation of the convertible legend makes the new SL an object of art by itself. However, quite contrary to the artist's unique creation, the new SL combines all functional and technical elements in an attractive shape.

It all started 35 years ago, when the legendary Mercedes SL was first presented to the public. Since then, the "SL virus" has been proliferating. And when as early as the 1970s the first drafts for the new SL

Another full-size epowood model. The roof is shown here in its final form. The roof went through 34 versions in its development phases before arriving at this result.

generation of the 90s were made, the Mercedes-Benz designers right from the start set their stakes very high: "We wanted to establish a stylistically consistent link with the enthralling first SL from the very beginning. We wanted to create a worthy successor to the aesthetically appealing 300 SL of the 1950s."

The first studies on a successor to the SL which had its first public appearance in 1971, were realized as early as 1973 and 1975. At that time, the entire field of sports car engineering was sounded out. The Mercedes designers remember that they had even designed a mid-engine concept.

It was as late as 1982 that constructive and directed work on the R 107 successor was resumed. Work groups within the design department allocated in the Sindelfingen Mercedes-Benz plant set to work with "almost uncontainable enthusiasm".

It was the purpose of the first stage to pursue in three main design directions: conventional drafts as the consistent continuation of the 107 model; futuristic-progressive drafts; dynamic drafts as the further development of the SL concept in the shape of a completely new yet in itself homogeneous design concept with a touch of tradition.

Today, we have before us the product of the third development approach. An SL

At last, here is the SL in its production configuration. The hood is an "intermediate" solution between the coupé and roadster versions. It provides almost perfect insulation from the climate and can be folded back in a few seconds thanks to the sophisticated electrically-operated mechanism.

Bird's eye-view of the hard-top SL. Produced in light alloy the hard-top weighs only thirty-four kilos, ten less than the one which fitted the previous SLs.

sports car in its own rights, a piece of design history, stylistically independent of its predecessor yet integrating neatly into the historically grown SL ideology. Characteristic features are the long bonnet conveying the impression of dynamic power, the compact roof design of both the hard and the soft top, with steeply inclined roof pillars as well as a compact, soft-contoured rear. The car's outline alone with fully retracted roof or with the soft or hard top in position, instantly conveys the fascinating spell of the SL.

During the entire styling process, nearly twenty models were built on a scale of 1:5. So were several clay and wood or plastic models on a scale of 1:1.

The roof design posed particular difficulties during the development of the R 129. For the new SL was declared the safest convertible sports car of the world when it was still on the drawing board.

The desire to achieve maximum safety, suitability to even the worst of weather conditions and unique comfort brought forth no less than 34 different roof concepts, among them a finned roof, which had a rigid roll-over bar, however. The solution arrived at in the end including a sensor-controlled retractable roll-over bar, is not a compromise but a synthesis of the best proposals. The designers did not neglect the safety aspect, for the roll-over bar, often derogatively called "handle" in many sports cars and convertibles, constitutes no disturbance factor whatsoever with respect to the aesthetic appearance of the new SL, but is an attractive matter of course.

Since 1985, no major alterations have been made to the design of the SL, although the Mercedes-Benz designers are known for their meticulous and untiring work, something they are very proud of: "In our workshops we modify and refine until time runs out and nothing can be improved any more".

Details

The compelling attraction of the new SL proves with what meticulous care the designers set to work. For an SL – apart from its purely stylistic features – traditionally has to meet requirements which lie rather in the psychological field of perception. And the SL in particular has always occupied a special position as far as the stylistic elements of a model family are concerned as innovative force and image leader and has always set the path for successive model series.

As far as the special character of the R 129 is concerned, it reflects on its owner. The SL coupé of 1989 is more than any other Mercedes a visualization of its distinctiveness. In other words: the human being was the main factor for the designers when drawing up the formal concept,

Bird's eye-view of the open SL. Even from such an unusual view it is easy to recognise the rigour in the roadster's lines and volumes, Mercedes-Benz style.

The Styling Centre took great pains to give the rear of the car an extremely sober and traditional elegance.

which was subsequently refined with scrupulous accuracy until meeting the exacting stylistic requirements.

It is an undisputable fact that apart from the purely aesthetic aspects values such as excellence, freedom, tradition, refinement, safety, reliability, prestige or simply success are ascribed to the new SL. The Mercedes designers have given the bodywork a marked air of superiority without much flexing of muscles. This is shown by the following brief summary of features.

The dynamic energy everybody expects of a Mercedes-Benz sports car is clearly expressed by the new SL. It has a very organic shape yet with a dynamic and definite – yet not forced flow of lines. This can be seen by the fact that eye-catching adornments such as spoilers, trim strips or aprons have been dispensed with. By means of subtle design features, the new SL embodies characteristics such as power potential on the one hand and calm elegance on the other. The characteristic design features of the new SL are conveyed much more discretely but leave an even more durable impression. Seen from the front, the new SL looks brawny, one could almost say ready to pounce like a beast of prey; seen from the side it presents itself in its long elegant shape, the rear is ingenuously rounded off. Some well-devised details such as the air vents integrated behind the front wheel arches clearly remind one of the times of the old SL and Mercedes racing cars.

Probably never before has discerning sportiness had such an appealing shape as the new SL. The neat elegance of the sides, which are without any beads, is most conspicuous. The upper edge of the body describes a smoothly flowing line, ascending towards the front windscreen, then dipping slightly at the doors before rising again to the rear. This line flow not only produces the subtle wedge shape but also makes for a homogeneous integration of the roof structure into the body base.

The organically integrated windscreen, the A-pillars which are inclined backwards, forming a smooth continuation of the front section behind the wheel arches – the roof is integrated in the dirt-deflecting system – the generously dimensioned side windows, which are nearly flush with the outer skin, as well as the slightly tapering rear pillars continuing the clear line flow towards the back, constitute an essential contribution to the overall design concept, rounding it off. The breadth of the vehicle, which is greatest across the rear wheel arches, and the strong yet smoothly tapering rear section make the SL look powerful, even brawny.

The long bonnet continues to be a symbol of SL classiness. Quite contrary to its predecessor, the R 107, the designers

This picture shows how the windscreen protects a considerable part of the cabin thanks to its steep rake (around 60°).

S SL 500

Left. Just the right rake, well joined to the two light clusters which set back a few millimetres, this radiator grille is perhaps one of the best-looking ones to come out of Stuttgart. Center. The side mirrors, of considerable size, are electrically adjusted, with memory storage for three-positions, and anti-fogging. Below. The front light clusters, which include the indicators, wrap round the side of the car to comply with American regulations. Note the small foglights.

The roll-bar (standard equipment on all models) is a harmonious part of the SL's design. Two sensors raise it automatically in the event of danger. The rear light clusters retain the characteristic anti-dirt moulding.

500 SL
S SL 500

The sports models of the Mercedes-Benz rang have the firm's badge, the three-pointed star, integrated into the grille. The SL's engines needed a lower supplementary air-intake, with the foglights set in at the ends.

catered for more even contours, not least in favour of improved aerodynamics. The result is a bonnet inclining smoothly towards the front, integrating the typical SL face with slightly stricter lines and the distinguished bumper to the effect that the entire front section melts into the overall shape of the bodywork.

The face and aerodynamics

The front is the most crucial appearance factor with symbolic content. Factors such as marque identity and product quality find their expression in the front view. This is why the inventors of the new SL consciously opted for the rather futuristic front end design which nevertheless looks familiar at first sight.

The newly-dimensioned SL radiator grille with its elegant contours is integrated into the refined framework at the front end of the low-reaching bonnet. And despite its newly-attained characteristic clear-cut shape it continues the tradition of the typical radiator grille of Mercedes-Benz racing cars and the predecessors of the new SL. This basic design can be traced back until the 1930s, as schematic drawings and photos show.

The grille of the new SL features modern design elements such as anodized aluminium louvres in titanium anthracite. Together with the logically integrated three-pointed star on the bonnet, the front

attains formal independence on the basis of its tradition.

Whereas the large three-pointed star and the wide chromium frame were prominent features in the face of the predecessor models, the R 129's star and radiator grille as "historic" design elements are complemented by louvres which are flush with the grille frame. Now, the star is no longer prominent but discretely yet distinctively decorates the grille, which is now slightly inclined towards the rear. The result of this inclination and the louvre arrangement is an advantageous air flow along the smooth front section and – together with the integrated headlamp design – increased pedestrian protection in the case of a collision.

The favourable aerodynamic body design is a striking feature of the new SL. Measures towards the perfection of the outer shape in the wind tunnel were jointly decided upon by the aerodynamics and the design department. Meticulous care was taken of the fact that the exclusiveness of the design was not sacrificed at the cost of spectacular and possibly not too well-weighed features. This is how – in consideration of all relevant criteria – extraordinary aerodynamic quality has been achieved, making the SL not only one of the most distinctive but also one of the aerodynamically most efficient sports cars in the

From this view the sharp tapering of the rear can be seen. This is the most traditional part of the model, with its vertical and horizontal lines. The two seats are also well-protected from behind, something not traditionally associated with a roadster. This Is a guarantee of safety as well as of comfort. The boot takes three suitcases.

world. Here a few examples of aerodynamic design measures: newly-dimensioned smooth-surfaced radiator grille inclined towards the rear; rounded-off bonnet front end with smooth transitions; front aprons reaching low down with partial front spoilers and integrated fog lamps; careful sealing of the entire front section; harmoniously integrated outside mirrors; windows strongly tapering towards the roof; new A-pillar design with optimized dirt water deflection; half-recessed door handles; smooth-surfaced side panels with concave entrance panels; rear section tapering strongly towards the back.

The bumpers, the windows and the ligths

For the first time ever a new bumper design was able to be realized on the new SL with invisible shock-absorbing elements. By means of this measure the bumpers appear perfectly even-surfaced.

The large-surfaced windows, which are almost flush with the outer skin as well as the windscreen inclined at an angle of just under 60° are striking features. The hard top rear window with an angle of approximately 65° is almost plain, hence emphasizing the sporty coupé character when seen directly from behind. With the three-part rear window in the soft top, good visibility is achieved.

The headlamp arrangement is reminiscent of earlier sports car generations: for

the first time, the upper edge of the grille is located slightly below the level of the headlamp unit, and the indicator lamps reach even further round the sides than was the case with the R 107 predecessor model. At the rear, too, the indicator lamps – which are ribbed again so as to ensure greater dirt deflection – wrap around the sides.

Conclusion

All these individual measures together with an appealing overall shape and top-class engineering come to form a perfect entity: the new Mercedes-Benz SL. This new SL furnishes further proof of the leading role Mercedes-Benz design plays in the automotive world. There are certain styling principles underlying the work of the Mercedes-Benz designers.

Technical functions and traditional values meet in an aesthetic shape to form a convincing symbiosis.

Il was only in this way that the new Mercedes-Benz SL was able to become not the stylistic fashionable end in itself but the characterful new SL. Powerful in its appearance yet with amazingly compact dimensions. Although the new-generation SL opens up new design dimensions, it remains true to the design philosophy characteristic of Mercedes-Benz.

km/h
l/100km
km
REST

Comfort

An abundance of comfort-enhancing features has been incorporated in the new series, among them the electro-hydraulically operated soft top, the front seats with integrated seat belts, a newly designed dust filter which cleans fresh air before it enters the interior, and an additional heating system which operates when the engine is switched off. Another new feature is a screen which wards off unpleasant draught in open driving. Over and above this, comfort is, of course, also determined by the engine's smooth running, the noise of air flow around the bodywork and the car's vibration and suspension behaviour. Intelligent solutions had to be found to the problem of meeting the self-imposed exacting demands on comfort in an open car.

The interior

The successful design of the SL bodywork with its elegant and classic sportiness arouses high expectations of the interior. And the question is: does the interior meet these expectations?

The first getting in, the first direct "feel" and all doubts are dispersed.

Its sportiness is stressed in combination with the clearly layed-out instrument panel, the neat line flow of the entire cockpit and the check seat covers and side and floor linings. The layout of the instrument cluster with five classic analog displays, lying in the driver's immediate field of vision, has been made even clearer by means of arranging every display instrument separately. Integrated in the even-surfaced centre console, called "dome" by the Mercedes designers, are all operating elements in a burr walnut panelling, conveying an impression of calm elegance as well as giving it a touch of high-tech.

Appointment features such as nozzles, glove compartment and oddments tray lids have been grouped together to form a generous entity conveying sporty elegance. The instrument panel ensures the highest possible impact safety. For this

The instruments are very clearly legible. The bars at 75, 123 and 193 kph represent top speed in respective gears. The illustration here is of the 500 SL, and they refer to the 4-speed automatic gearbox.

The sophisticated hood operating system only takes 30 seconds from start to finish. It can only be activated when the car is standing still. A warning light signals that the hood is correctly locked.

The SL's cabin. Standard trim is velvet, and leather is available on request. The use of wood gives the car a richer look and provides a psychological effect of comfort and warmth.

reason, the Mercedes designers and engineers have avoided to integrate more wood trim elements.

Above the centre air nozzle, a spectacles box and the trip computer display (with automatic adjustment to the prevailing light conditions) are located. The operating switches for the automatic heating system, temperature control and air conditioning have been redesigned as well.

The functionality and aesthetic appeal of the seats plays a prominent role in the overall impression conveyed by the interior. The SL seats, completely new in their design, integrate harmoniously into the overall interior set up just as every other appointment feature. For the first time ever, there is no gap between the seat and the adjoining function element, both parts forming a concordant entity. Behind the seats, the roll-over bar – whether up or down-fits neatly into the overall design, hence continuing the line flow of the bodywork and interior.

Many of the comfort-enhancing features are included in the standard specifications, for instance electric windows, central locking and the electrically adjustable steering column in the 300 SL-24 and 500 SL.

In addition, other features are optionally available. Among these is a memory feature for electric seat, mirror and steering column adjustment. Once the driver has adjusted the seat, the mirrors and the steering column to the ergonomically optimum positions, he only has to press one of the memory keys to record this setting. After a change in position, the programmed setting for seat, mirrors and steering column can be recalled at the push of a key.

The standard central locking system has been refined by the addition of an "internal locking" feature. This locks all the lockable compartments inside the car – from the spectacles box to the luggage space. A total of six compartments can be centrally locked and thus secured against theft even when the car is open.

Operational comfort is further enhanced by the optionally available infrared remote control unit for the central locking system. The doors can be locked from a distance of up to 6 metres by pressing a transmitter key. For safety reasons, every SL with infrared transmitter is given a different basic signal. In addition, every time the keys are pressed, a different code, ruled by a special algorithm, is transmitted. This virtually prevents other transmitters from taking effect. Open side windows can be closed both by means of the infrared transmitter and by turning the door locking key.

Fresh-air filter

The most noteworthy new feature of the efficient ventilation system is a so-called Elektrete filter which effectively cleans the ambient air drawn in by the blower. The filtering is effected by matting whose polycarbonate fibres are electrostatically charged during the spinning process; the filter completely captures pollen and dust particles as well as liquid particles down to a size of 5 micrometres. It also traps up to 60% of particles which are ten times smaller, for instance bacteria, industrial dust, soot and smog. Depending on the degree of soiling, the filter must be replaced during servicing or at least once a year. Since the air channelling and blower output have been improved, the air flow rate is higher than in the predecessor model, in spite of the air filter. Automatic climate control operates in different modes, depending on whether the roof is opened or closed. This ensures that the heating is controlled largely automatically even with the soft top down.

Interior heating even with the engine switched off

To keep the interior comfortably warm even when the engine is switched off, the residual heat of the engine is used to heat the interior, for instance at level crossings, at traffic lights, in traffic jams or during a quick stop off at the shops. By pressing the "Rest" key, an electric circulation pump is activated which channels the hot engine coolant through the heating system's heat exchanger. Air quantity and distribution are automatically controlled. The circulation pump switches off after thirty minutes at the latest so that the engine can be restarted reliably.

Low-vibration bodywork

In the design of the new SL, Mercedes-Benz set itself the task of creating a convertible with particularly low vibrations and high torsional rigidity. In extensive tests of the completely newly developed bodywork, it was determined where, how and what additional reinforcements were required to stabilise the open bodywork.

The safety belts are integral with the seats. They have belt tensioners which only go into action in the event of a frontal impact which generates greater deceleration force than normal.

These investigations led to the use of additional struts which ensure a higher overall rigidity of the bodywork. In the front section of the car, two profiled struts, fitted with their own vibration dampers, link the front axle carrier with the door sills. In the rear, two tubular struts link the door sills with the spare wheel recess. As a consequence, bodywork distortion of the new SL is as low as that of the Mercedes saloons and coupés which means that the torsional rigidity of the SL bodywork has been noticeably increased, giving exceptionally good vibration behaviour for a car of this type.

Soft top and light-weight hard top

The standard specifications of the new SL include an electro-hydraulically operated soft top and a removable hard top. Both versions can be operated and handled effortlessly.

At the push of a button, it takes thirty seconds for the soft top to be folded away or to be extended and locked. At the same time, the side windows and the roll-over bar are lowered and subsequently return to their original positions.

Sophisticated technology is required to achieve this ease of operation. The energy required to open and close the soft top is supplied by an electrically driven hydraulic pump which is accommodated, together with the oil reservoir, in the spare

Close-up of the door controls (above) and electrical seat adjuster (below). There are three memory positions which include the driving mirrors.

wheel recess. The opening and closing is controlled by a micro-processor and monitored by 17 proximity switches; the hydraulic system employs 15 pressure cylinders and 11 solenoid valves.

It goes without saying that a squeeze-in protection system is incorporated just as well as manual emergency control. In "off" position, the hydraulic system is depressurised, and all the relevant points are mechanically locked.

The soft top can be extended and retracted only when the car is stationary and the ignition switched on. The soft top frame components keep the roof firmly under control. A specially shaped strut serves as a folding aid and prevents the soft top fabric from lifting off the frame ("ballooning"). Several steel ropes which tension the closed soft top also hold the fabric taut even at high speeds.

The interior roof lining can be replaced easily and is specially coated on the inside; together with meticulously designed roof frame sealing, this goes a long way towards keeping noise levels down.

The noise of air flow around the car, which is generally somewhat louder in a convertible, has been reduced to a minimum by means of careful coordination of form and function in the wind tunnel.

Open driving at high speeds inevitably causes draught which feels unpleasant around the head and neck, and which ruffles the occupants' hair and clothes. To make driving at higher speeds nonetheless enjoyable and to increase safety, Mercedes-Benz offers an optionally available draught-stop which does not detract from the pleasure of driving an open car. This draught-stop is a framed screen which can easily and quickly be fastened to the roll-over bar. With the draught-stop in upright position, draught and wind noises are minimised, and the interior can be effectively heated even during the colder season, so that driving the new SL with the soft top down is possible much more frequently.

A hard top weighing only 34 kilos

The standard hard top is made of light alloy and weighs only 34 kilos – 10 kilos less than the predecessor's roof. It can be removed and re-installed easily and effortlessly. The roof is locked at four points, and in addition safely located at two points. The roof is locked electromagnetically via a central switch. The inside of the hard top has a self-supporting sandwich-type plastic lining which absorbs noises and provides efficient insulation against heat and cold.

Left. The automatic gear lever with the distinctive selector gate. Below, the controls to open and shut the hood, also used to fit the hard-top, and the right window control.

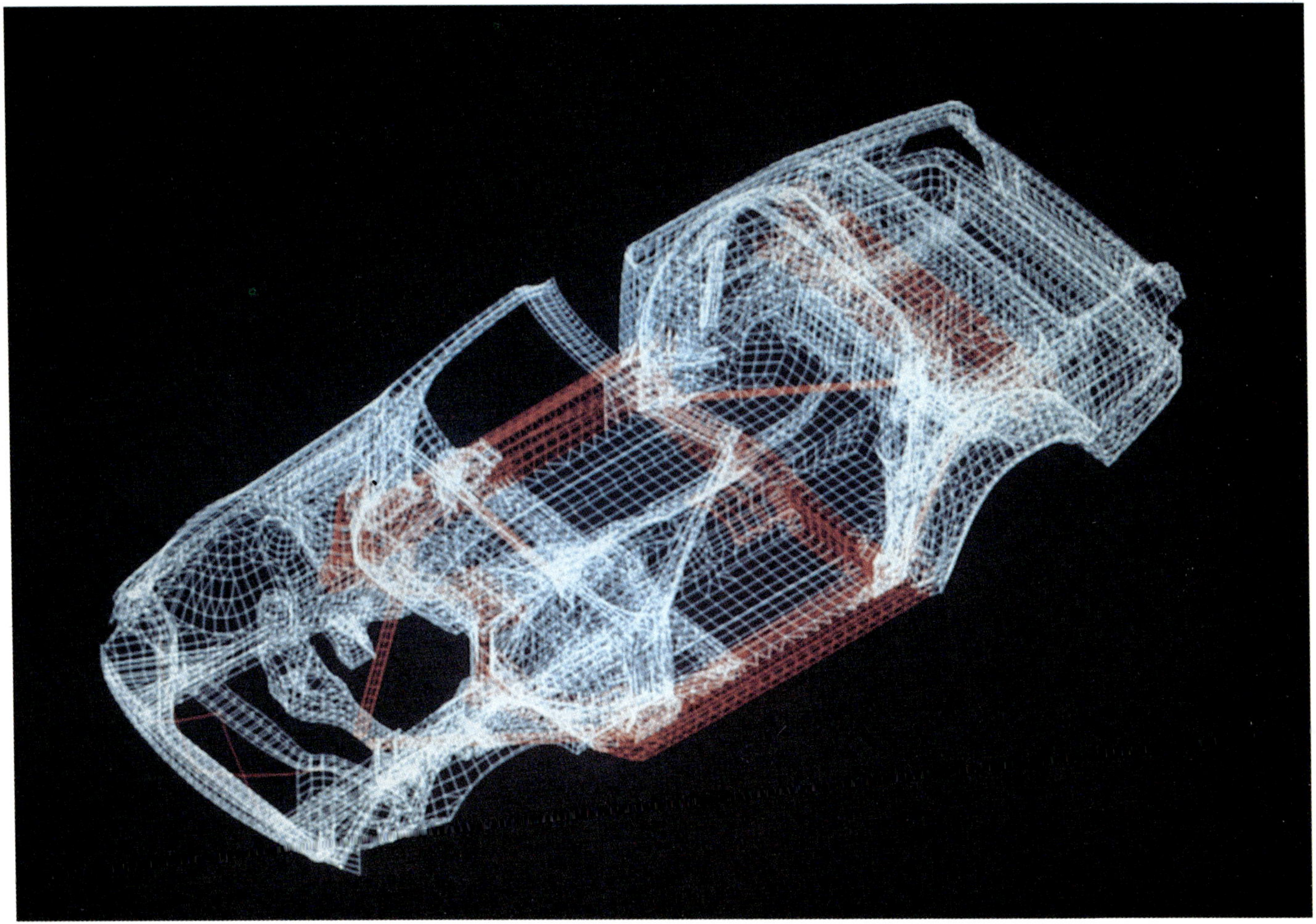

MECHANICS AND SAFETY

Three powerful engines

In engine technology, Mercedes-Benz sets new standards with a refined emission control system and automatic camshaft adjustment, the latter improving the new four-valve engine's smooth running characteristics and raising its torque. The new SL is available with either of three high-capacity and smooth-running engines which are quite different in their performance characteristics: 3-litre 6-cylinder 2-valve in-line engine, 140 kW/190 HP; 3-litre 6-cylinder 4-valve in-line engine, 170 kW/231 HP; 5-litre 4-valve V8 engine, 240 kW/326 HP.

The cars are fitted as standard with the closed-loop three-way catalytic converter. In addition, fuel vapours from the tank are conveyed via an activated charcoal filter back to the engine for combustion.

Modified 3-litre 6-cylinder 2-valve engine

The 3-litre 6-cylinder 2-valve engine is largely identical with the well-known power unit which is also installed in the Mercedes-Benz W124-class.

A new feature of this engine is the "open" combustion chamber. To ensure more efficient combustion of the fuel/air mixture, there is no longer a quench zone in the cylinder head. This intensifies combustion and thus lowers the raw emission of unburnt hydrocarbons.

Engines with catalytic converter are fitted with an air pump which channels additional fresh air through the cylinder head and injects it into the exhaust ports where it is mixed with hot exhaust gases. The afterburning process of the exhaust gases, which starts immediately after the engine is started, accounts for lower pollutant emission even at this stage. Over and above this, this process improves the conditions for subsequent catalytic emission control. Nox emissions are reduced by means of exhaust gas recirculation, a standard feature.

All detail improvements to the cylinder head, a modified camshaft and the double-fluted catalytic converter account for im-

CAD/CAM image of the SL's body.

The 3-litre 6-cylinder 12-valve engine. Output 190 HP at 5700 rpm.

proved torque and engine output ratings and even smoother running characteristics.

New 3-litre 6-cylinder 4-valve engine

The 3-litre 6-cylinder 4-valve engine shares a large number of components with the 6-cylinder 2-valve engine. A completely new development is its 4-valve cylinder head with inlet camshaft adjustment.

The valves, fitted at an angle of 50° and arranged in compact, pent-roof shape combustion chambers with level pistons and centrally positioned spark plugs, are actuated by one inlet camshaft and one outlet camshaft via maintenance-free hydraulic bucket tappets. The two camshafts are driven by a duplex roller chain.

Camshaft adjustment, a new feature used for the first time by Mercedes-Benz, improves the cylinders' volumetric efficiency in dependence of engine speed and torque, resulting in improved idling and higher torque. Furthermore, the generously dimensioned intake and exhaust ports, arranged according to the cross-flow principle and converging inside the cylinder head, account for low gas cycle resistances.

The ports are arranged too as to provide for the optimum positioning of the injection nozzle relative to the cylinder for good cold-starting behaviour. The insulated

nozzle brackets are airbathed so as to ensure reliable hot-starting.

Furthermore, special intake manifold seals prevent the injection valves from being heated up.

To minimise noise emission even at this engine's high specific output, the pistons are sprayed with engine oil from below. The oil reduces piston temperature, thus ensuring unchanging piston clearances. This significantly improves piston lubrication and thus reduces noise emission.

As in the 6-cylinder 2-valve engine, the 4-valve unit's exhaust emissions are reduced by means of a closed-loop three-way catalytic converter, additional fresh-air injection into the exhaust ports and exhaust gas recirculation.

The single-part cylinder head has sufficient rigidity for valve train support and combustion chamber stabilisation, in spite of its low weight. Fitted with the proven crank assembly, this engine is an exceptionally dynamic unit with a maximum engine speed of 7000/rpm. A torque of over 250 Nm is on tap over a broad engine speed band, from 3000 to 6500/rpm and the four-valve engine's maximum torque of 272 Nm is reached at 4600/rpm.

The optimised four-valve engine is fitted with a combined mechanical-electronic fuel injection system which, because of its capacity, is also used for the V8 engine.

The 3-litre 6-cylinder 24-valve engine. Output 231 HP at 6300 rpm.

New 5-litre 4-valve V8 engine

The most powerful engine for the new SL is a 5-litre V8 unit whose increased power output is predominantly due to its improved gas cycle employing a total of 32 valves.

The cylinder crankcase of the new 4-valve engine has been derived from the proven M 117 S-class engine. Its high power output of 240 kW/326 HP has been achieved by means of substantial modifications to the light-alloy unit.

The iron-coated pistons and the cylinder contact surfaces form a low-wear combination. The crankshaft is forged out of high-strength, micro-alloyed tempered steel, with all radii being additionally hardened.

The two cylinder heads, equipped with 32 valves and four camshafts, have been completely newly developed. Two inlet and two outlet camshafts, jointly driven by a duplex roller chain, actuate the valves via maintenance-free hydraulic bucket tappets. The valves are asymmetrically positioned at an angle of 37.7° relative to the cylinder axis. With the steeply angled position of the exhaust valves, the V8 engine could be kept rather small in width. This large-capacity four-valve engine, too, is fitted with electronically controlled inlet camshaft adjustment, developed by Mercedes-Benz. This improves the cylinders' volumetric efficiency, and thus torque, power output and idling.

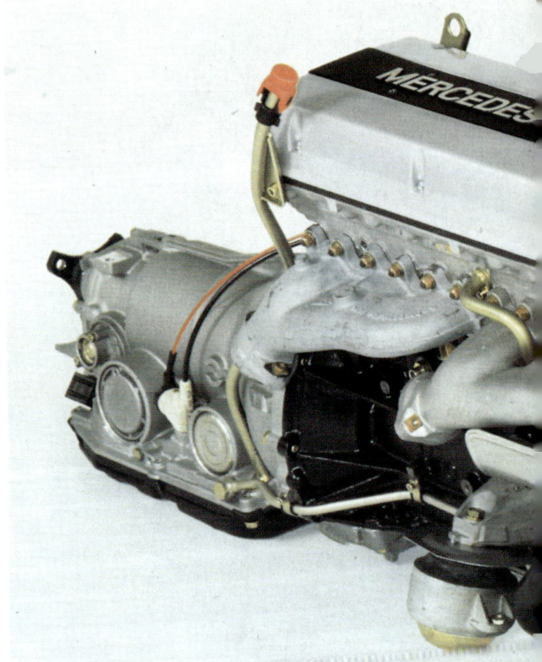

Because of the higher oil flow rate in the four-valve cylinder heads, each cylinder is fitted with a separate oil return passage. Two oil splash shields in the oil sump reduce oil foaming, which can damage the hydraulic bucket tappets. The compact, pent-roof shape combustion chamber with centrally positioned spark plug has been optimised with a view to flame propagation. Short flame travel and defined turbulences account for optimum energy utilisation, knock resistance and low raw emissions. The electronic injection and ignition systems, exhaust gas recirculation control and the air injection into the exhaust ports correspond to the six-cylinder four-valve engine's systems in terms of design and function.

Automatic camshaft adjustments

A rigid camshaft with non-adjustable ignition timing will always constitute a compromise with a view to torque on the one hand and peak performance on the other. With inlet camshaft adjustment, now introduced by Mercedes-Benz, individual valve overlap in the four-valve engine is now modified according to the engine's operation condition. Hence, with the new four-valve technology from Mercedes-Benz compromise is a thing of the past.

With automatic inlet camshaft adjustment, there is virtually no valve overlap at idle speed, accounting for smoother runn-

The 5-litre 8-cylinder 32-valve engine. Output 326 HP at 5500 rpm.

ing and reduced pollutant emission and fuel consumption.

At medium engine speeds, greater valve overlap at TDC improves the cylinders' volumetric efficiency and raises the torque. For high output ratings at high engine speeds, the closing of the inlet valves is delayed.

Inlet camshaft adjustment is controlled by the injection system's control unit in dependence of torque and engine speed. The adjustment mechanism proper, however, is fitted in the camshaft gear.

The camshaft gear continues to be fitted on the camshaft and is driven by the crankshaft via a roller chain. A new feature is the ability of the camshaft to turn relative to the camshaft gear.

At the front end of the camshaft with longitudinal toothing, an adjustment piston with helical outer toothing is fitted which meshes with the inner helical toothing of the camshaft gear. Depending on the position of the piston, the position of the camshaft relative to the camshaft gear can thus be altered, thus changing the valve timing by the inlet camshaft.

To change the position of the adjustment piston, a magnet activated by the injection system's electronic unit operates a valve, thus forcing in engine oil which moves the piston into the desired position. The camshaft is simultaneously adjusted via the helical toothing.

KE5: a new injection system

More exacting demands made on the injection and ignition system's electronic control units call for greater computer capacity. Hence, each system has its own control unit. These units are, however, linked by means of an interface so that data can be exchanged. It has thus become possible to incorporate additional engine management functions. Over and above this, the previous functions can be performed more efficiently and in a more intelligent manner, and finally, networking also provides for the redundancy of the most important sensors.

The new KE 5 injection system operates mechanically-electronically. Fuel metering is effected by means of a fuel distributor activated by an electronic control unit.

The additional functions now incorporated in particular reduce pollutant emissions: oxygen sensor heating increases operational reliability and service life; an intermittent cold-starting aid provides for fuel enrichment orientated towards requirements; the injection system's control unit also monitors and controls exhaust gas recirculation and additional air injection; in the event of failure of important sensors, the electronic unit feeds in a replacement value, thus maintaining operational reliability; fuel tank venting: the fuel vapours from the tank are passed through an ac-

MERCEDES-BENZ

X-ray view of the 500 SL, showing all the mechanicals. The sophisticated hood and roll-bar mechanisms can be seen at the back.

tivated charcoal filter and mixed with the combustion gases at specified intervals. The venting of the activated charcoal filter is controlled by the electronic unit; engine parameter data are recorded, ensuring optimum control for instance when re-starting the engine.

Example: fuel apportionment in accordance with ambient air pressure may vary, depending on whether the car is driven down in a valley or high up in the mountains. When the engine is re-started, the electronic system will "remember" at what altitude the car was parked and apportion the appropriate fuel quantity for smooth starting.

Exemplary reduction in pollutant emission

A large number of new and additional technical features have been incorporated in the SL engines to reduce pollutant emission as early as the combustion stage.

Among these features is a V-belt-driven air pump. During warm-up, it injects fresh air through the cylinder head and into the exhaust ports. This accounts for the after-burning of unburnt hydrocarbons and carbon monoxide directly at the exhaust valves. In this way, emissions are reduced, and the catalytic converter heats up more quickly. All SL engines are equipped with additional exhaust gas recirculation.

Since the cylinder head of the 6-cylinder 2-valve engine no longer has a quench zone, the fuel/air mixture is burnt more thoroughly, resulting in reduced raw emissions of unburnt hydrocarbons.

Inlet camshaft adjustment in the four-valve engines also contributes to a reduction in the raw emission of unburnt hydrocarbons and nitrogen oxides.

The SL models' broad tunnel accommodates a completely newly developed double-fluted catalytic converter with two ceramic monoliths fitted side by side in a single housing. This new design yields the following advantages: high engine output thanks to large catalytic converter cross-section; high long-term stability and emission quality consistency; low noise emission through optimised mixing areas.

Modified transmissions

The two 6-cylinder models are fitted as standard with a 5-speed manual gearbox matched to the powerful engines. Top speed is reached in fifth gear. The 300 SL-24 is optionally available with a manual gearbox with ratios which lend themselves to a sporty driving style. The ratio in fifth gear is 1:1, thus fifth gear is not an overdrive. The driver is able to change through the gears quickly since second and third gear and fourth and fifth gear are in the same plane respectively. Comfort is enhanced by the fact that reverse is fully synchronised.

In conjunction with the 5-speed manual

gearbox, a two-mass flywheel is installed for more effective damping of power train vibrations.

The proven 4-speed automatic transmission is optionally available for the two 6-cylinder models and standard on the 500 SL. The ratios of this transmission, too, have been matched to the higher engine output ratings.

New features on the automatic transmission are a display for the selector lever position and a special parking lock.

The locking is effected by an additional mechanism with a Bowden cable which connects the steering lock with the selector lever. It is thus ensured that the ignition key can only be removed after the selector lever has been put into "P" position. Conversely, the selector lever can only be moved into another position when the ignition key has been inserted and turned.

Sporty performance

The engines and transmission ratios have been designed for sporty performance in keeping with the new SL models' characteristics. Because of its engine power, the 500 SL would be capable of effortlessly reaching top speeds above 250 km/h yet various electronic features have been incorporated to limit the top speed in the interest of safety, for instance with a view to tyre capacity.

The performance of all models has been markedly improved compared with the previous models – the new 300 SL-24, for instance, outstrips the previous 420 SL.

Safety

The new Mercedes-Benz convertible is a sporty car which at the same time features a high standard of comfort. In suspension design, sophisticated solutions have been achieved, tailored to the characteristics of an open two-seater and meeting the most exacting demands on handling and ride.

The most significant contribution towards active safety is rendered by good handling and ride characteristics. This requires first and foremost excellent suspension with precise yet shock-absorbing wheel location elements. For the new SL series, therefore, the proven combination of shock absorber strut independent front suspension and multi-link independent rear suspension has been retained. A new feature, meeting even more exacting demands, is the adaptive damping system (ADS). The proven acceleration skid control (ASR) and automatic locking differential (ADS) are also available for the new SL. These electronically controlled and automatically operating systems relieve the driver from stress and thus improve handling and physiological safety as well as the ease of control.

A car's road-holding stability is predominantly accounted for by its rear axle.

Diagram showing the Adaptive Damping System (ADS). Five sensors send messages to the electronic control unit which controls the damper settings.

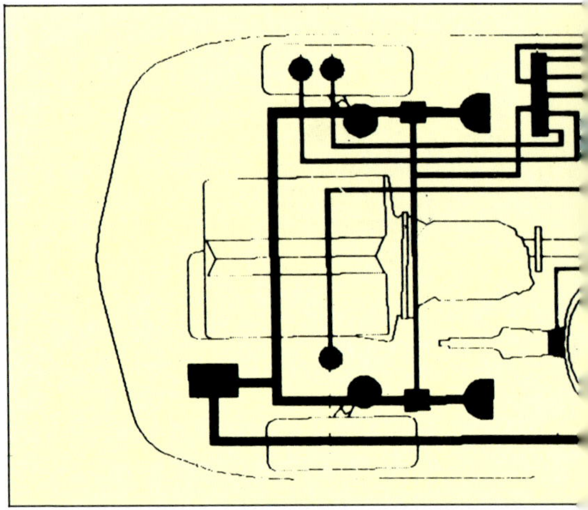

This is not least the reason why Mercedes-Benz put so much engineering effort into rear axle design. The multi-link independent rear suspension, tried and tested in the compact and mid-series models, continues to set standards for precise wheel location, thanks to the three-dimensional arrangement of the five links which under spring compression only permit minor, precisely defined kinematic steering effects. In addition, the elasticities (displacements) in the link mounts are tuned so as to prevent toe-in changes at the wheel under longitudinal forces, thus ensuring good straight-line stability. The steering response under lateral forces (cornering for instance) is also precisely defined. In its effectiveness, the SL's multi-link independent rear suspension is comparable to passive rear-wheel steering.

Automatic damping and level control

The engineers worked on an even further-going, uncompromising solution, the adaptive damping system (ADS) launched for the first time in the SL series. On the move, ADS permanently adapts the damper characteristics to the requirements at any given point in time. The change-over from one damper setting to another – there are altogether four, from soft to hard – takes place fully automatically and imperceptibly.

In the design of a car's suspension system, the engineer is confronted with the problem of reconciling two objectives which due to the laws of physics conflict, namely maximum safety versus optimum comfort. A car can be said to have comfortable suspension if vertical body acceleration on an uneven road surface remains sufficiently limited. To this end, the wheels must be capable of easily evading an obstacle by moving upwards – which calls for soft springing and damping. Because of the wheels' inertia mass, however, such a softly damped movement will bring about great load variations at the wheel, causing wheel bounce under extreme conditions.

It is at this point that the conflict with

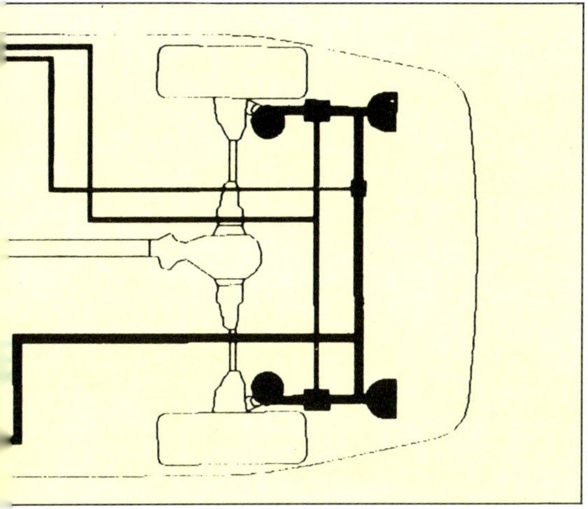

safety arises because the latter calls for the smallest possible dynamic wheel load variations.

In the interest of optimum comfort, a soft damper setting is chosen in straight-ahead driving over a road with only minor unevenness. On undulations, however, the ADS provides firm damping in order to prevent pitching. Upon receiving signals indicating an evasive manoeuvre or cornering, the system changes in time to a harder damper setting, even before lateral acceleration to any extent worth mentioning occurs, thus minimising wheel load variations. This illustrates the philosophy behind ADS: the damper setting provides for optimum ride comfort whenever comparatively little lateral stability is required, for instance in "normal" straight-ahead driving. As soon as lateral stability is called for, however (for cornering for instance), ADS changes over to firm damping – virtually in an anticipating manner in the case of steering manoeuvres – so as to provide maximum safety reserves under all conditions. The damping is also adjusted to the appropriate "hard" setting under sharp acceleration and braking and also when the car is heavily laden, in order to improve road-holding stability.

Five sensors are permanently monitoring the driving condition. They record vertical acceleration of wheel and bodywork, road speed, steering wheel angle and load. An electronic control unit processes the sensor signals, calculates the optimum damper setting at any given point in time, and activates the solenoid valves in the suspension's hydraulic system, the damper setting being modified by the opening or closing of these solenoid valves.

ADS is coupled with automatic level adjustment and control. The latter ensures that the car remains at a constant level, at all four wheels and irrespective of the load and its distribution. At speeds above 120 kph, the bodywork is automatically lowered by 15 mm to increase road-holding stability and reduce drag. To increase ground clearance, the driver can raise the

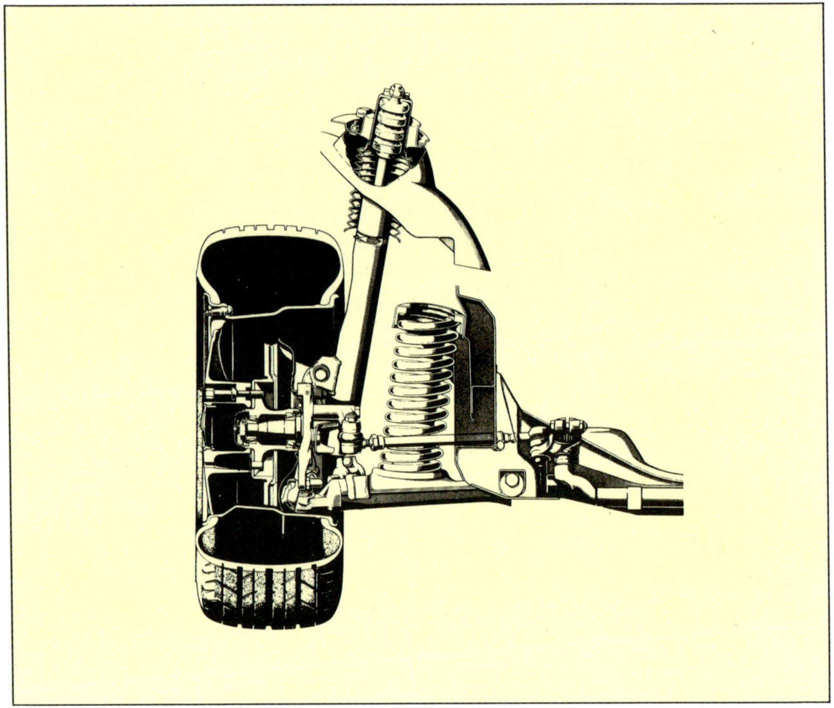

Section drawing of the front wheel and relative suspension.

car's level by 30 mm – however, only up to a speed of approx. 80 kph. If this speed is exceeded, the car is automatically lowered to its normal level.

Reliable brakes

At a very early stage in design, it emerged that compliance with Mercedes-Benz's own safety standards for brake reliability and brake power reserves in a car of this performance category would call for wheel brakes which could hardly be accommodated in conventional 15-inch wheels. For this reason, the new SLs are fitted with 16-inch wheels. All four wheels are decelerated by generously dimensioned disc brakes, the front brake discs being internally ventilated. The light-alloy rims, size 8Jx16, are fitted with 225/55 ZR 16 tyres. The anti-lock braking system (ABS) is a standard feature.

Passive safety

At Mercedes-Benz, vehicle occupant protection is traditionally a matter of top priority. This philosophy, which has been applied in the design and production of several generations of cars, has led to the development of many very important safety features which have created automotive history. These include the anti-lock braking system (ABS) – a feature developed and introduced into production by Mercedes-Benz – in addition to the airbag and the seat-belt tensioner.

The raisable roll-over bar

Thanks to the raisable roll-over bar, a completely new feature, the classical appearance of the open car has been retained. When retracted, the roll-over bar is located in front of the soft-top compartment. It has two modes of operation: crash activation and comfort activation. In other words, it can also be extended slowly if desired; the driver merely has to operate a switch, the actual work being performed by a spring-loaded hydraulic mechanism. In crash activation, the roll-over bar extends extremely rapidly in potentially dangerous situations without any action on the part of the driver. The spring components are then disengaged by the hydraulic system so that the roll-over bar can quickly reach its end position.

Crash activation also occurs if the driver selects the comfort mode in a hazardous situation. The bar can also be returned to its original position at the touch of a switch. This procedure is taken care of by the hydraulic system, whereby the spring mechanism is tensioned.

In crash activation, the roll-over bar extends within the space of about 0.3 seconds, with an average speed of about 1 m/s. Since the bar is fully padded with polyurethane, possible contact with rear-seat passengers cannot cause injury.

Section drawing of the rear wheel and relative suspension.

Automatic damping and level control.

The roll-over bar consists of a U-shaped tube of high-quality steel, which when extended rests on the robustly dimensioned centre pillar.

The integral seat for increased safety

A new generation of seats is now being introduced in the SL: Mercedes-Benz has developed an integral seat which does not have much in common with its predecessors.

This seat is based on a frame of pressure-diecast magnesium, which increases the transverse rigidity of the vehicle in a lateral collision.

The load-bearing frame has made it possible to incorporate the following functions into the fully electrically adjustable seat, thus enhancing safety and operational comfort: three-point inertia-reel seat belt; seat belt height adjustment; head restraint adjustment; seat-belt tensioner.

In this integrated occupant safety system, the seat-belt height adjustment is interconnected with the head restraint adjustment. Five electric motors move the seat squab and backrest into the most comfortable position, providing appropriate seat-belt heights and head restraint positions for people of various heights.

These comfort features also serve to enhance occupant protection. The belts fit optimally thanks to the individual sash guide height adjustment and the constant position of the lap strap.

The protective function of the seat belt is enhanced by means of an electronically activated seat-belt tensioner integrated into the seat, reducing belt slack.

A memory feature is available as an optional extra for storing electronic adjustment settings of the seat squab, backrest, head restraint positions and the seat-belt height.

The airbag (by request)

In a frontal collision, the protection afforded by the seat belts can be further enhanced by the airbags for the driver and front-seat passenger. The latter takes the place of the glove compartment.

The electronic "crash sensor", incorporating microprocessor technology, controls the activation of both the seat-belt tensioners and the airbags. In the event of a frontal collision, this control unit assesses the severity of the accident on the basis of the rate and duration of the vehicle's deceleration. If one or both of the programmed thresholds are exceeded, an electronic system transmits a command to ignite the gas generators. The seat-belt tensioners are activated as soon as the lower threshold is exceeded; if the upper threshold is also passed, the airbags for the driver and front-seat passenger also receive an activation command.

The airbag system is automatically

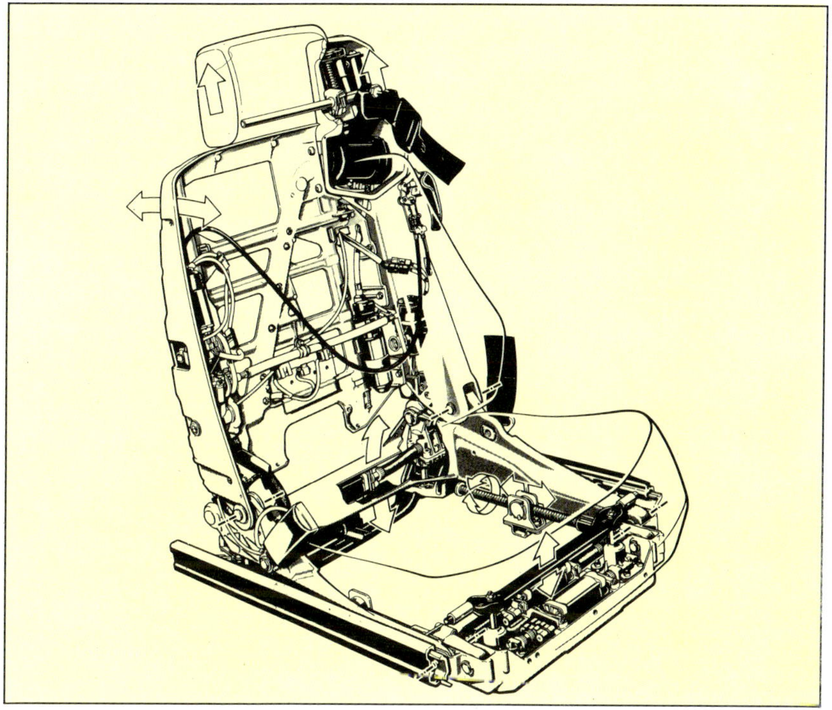

Structural drawing of the seat and seat belt.

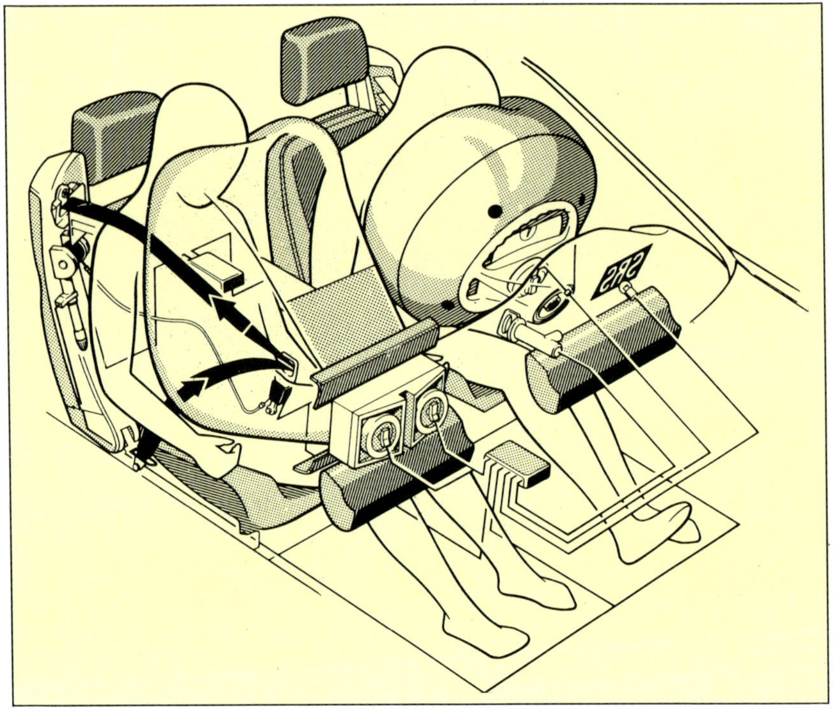

The air-bag, an optional, also protects the passenger.

tested every time the ignition is switched on and is continuously monitored when the car is in motion. The functional availability of the system is indicated by a control lamp.

Optimum occupant protection

All Mercedes-Benz safety design features are aimed at providing maximum protection for vehicle occupants. The crash tests must fulfil the following criteria: the passenger compartment must remain intact; the interior must incorporate large, energy-absorbing contact zones; the restraint systems must operate reliably; unproblematical rescuing of the occupants must be assured; the fuel system must be leakproof.

In all design measures, the protection of the occupant compartment is given absolute priority. Only when this basic requirement is met can safety features such as the restraint systems and padded contact areas completely fulfil their protective function.

As accident analyses have shown, vehicles are subject to an extremely high degree of structural stress in the course of accidents actually occurring. This degree of stress is not taken into account by any legislation either in Europe or in the Usa. This particularly applies to frontal collisions with oncoming traffic and with telegraph poles and to impacts to the rear, side and roof of the vehicle.

The preliminary evaluations and crash tests carried out prior to production have taken into account the structural peculiarities of the open vehicle and have led to the following design measures to alleviate the consequences of frontal collisions: an occupant compartment which retains its longitudinal rigidity even in an off-set frontal collision; absorption of some of the impact energy by the side of the front end not directly involved in the impact; spatial distribution of longitudinal forces from the front end to the occupant compartment via a specially developed yoke; preventing the penetration of components through the fire wall, especially into the driver's footwell; a minimum of steering system displacement; low repair costs.

In spite of the car's relatively short rear-end overhang, an above-average level of occupant protection has also been achieved for rear-end collisions.

Especially in lateral impacts, the occupant compartment is subject to extreme stresses. By means of a series of measures for increased transverse rigidity in the floor and seats, further improvements have been incorporated into the SL for this type of accident too.

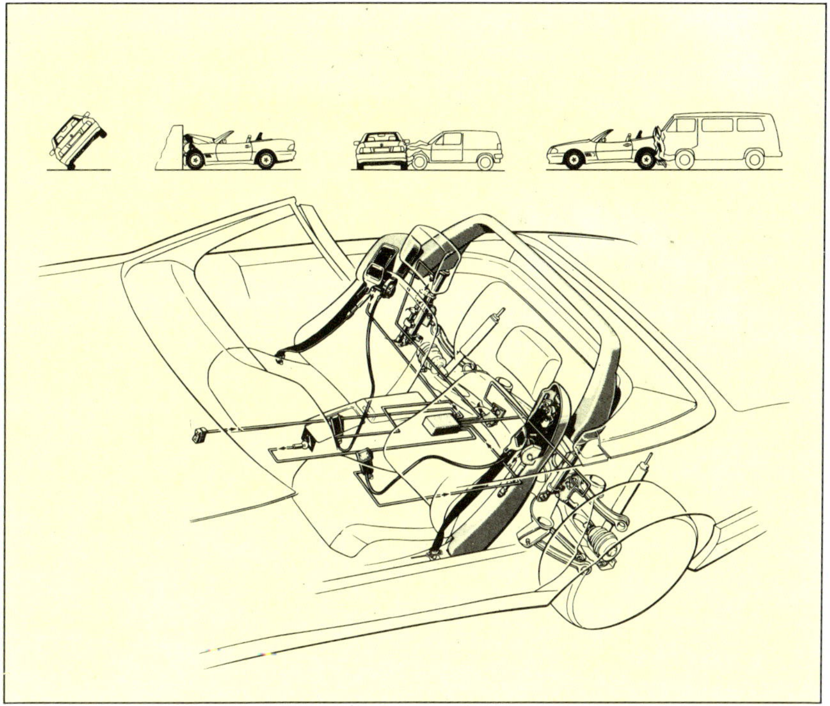

Diagram showing how the roll-bar works.

1
2
3
4
5
6
7
8
9
10
11
12
13
14
15
16
17
18
19
20
21
22
23
24
25
26
27
28
29
30
31
SRS
AIRBAG

1 - Swivelling air vent
2 - Headlamp beam control
3 - Light switch
4 - Handle for releasing parking brake
5 - Lever for opening bonnet
6 - Parking brake pedal
7 - Combination switch
8 - Cruise control/Tempomat
9 - Horn control
10 - Instrument cluster
11 - Steering lock with ignition/starter switch
12 - Swivelling air vent
13 - Stowage compartment
14 - Glovebox - illuminated in steering lock position 1 or 2 - not available on cars with front passenger airbag
15 - Thumbwheel for adjusting left-hand air vent
16 - Thumbwheel for adjusting centre air vent
17 - Thumbwheel for adjusting right-hand air vent
18 - Heater, air conditioning, automatic climate control
19 - Radio
20 - Heated rear screen
21 - Fanfare
22 - Hazard warning system
23 - Snow chain switch (vehicles equipped with acceleration skid control - ASR)
24 - Rollover bar switch
25 - Stowage compartment (press button down to open)
26 - Switch for adjusting mirrors
27 - Roof switch
28 - Electric window switches
29 - Heated seat switches
30 - Auxiliary heater
31 - Ashtray with cigarette lighter

ENGINE	300 SL	300 SL-24	500 SL	600 SL
Disposition:	longitudinal front			
Materials:	cylinder head and cylinder block light alloy			
Cylinders:	6 in-line	6 in-line	V8	V12
Bore and stroke:	88.5 x 80.2 mm	88.5 x 80.2 mm	96.5 x 85 mm	89 x 80.2 mm
Piston displacement:	2960 cc	2960 cc	4973 cc	5987 cc
Compression ratio:	9.2:1	10:1	10:1	10:1
Maximum power:	140 kW (190 HP) at 5700 rpm	170 kW (231 HP) at 6300 rpm	240 kW (326 HP) at 5700 rpm	300 kW (408 HP) at 5200 rpm
Maximum torque:	260 Nm at 4500 rpm	272 Nm at 4600 rpm	480 Nm at 3900 rpm	580 Nm at 3800 rpm
Timing system:	SOHC 2 valves per cylinder	DOHC, 4 valves per cylinder		
Fuel feed and ignition:	integral, Bosch KE Jetronic			Bosch LH Jetronic
Lubrication:	dry sump			
Cooling system:	front radiator, electric fan			
Anti-pollution system:	3-way catalytic converter			
DRIVELINE				
Drive:	rear-wheel			
Clutch:	dry single-plate		hydraulic torque converter	
Gearbox:	5-speed manual, on request 4-speed automatic		4-speed automatic	
Final ratio:	2.65	3.67	3.29	NA
Differential:	self-locking			
CAR BODY				
Type:	2-door, 2+2 seater roadster-coupé			

Frame:	all steel monoque			
Front suspension:	wishbones, gas pressure shock absorbers, coil springs, anti-roll bar			
Rear suspension:	multilink independent rear suspension with anti-squat and anti-lift control, gas pressure shock absorbers, coil springs, anti-roll bar			
Steering system:	power-assisted recirculating ballnut steering,			
Brakes:	discs, front self-vented, brake booster, progressively acting ABS			
Rims:	8J x 16			NA
Tyres:	225/55 R 16 Z			NA
Fuel tank:	80 lt			
DIMENSIONS AND WEIGHTS				
Length:	4470 mm			
Width:	1812 mm			
Height:	1293 mm			
Wheelbase:	2515 mm			
Front and rear tracks:	1535/1523 mm			NA
Kerb weight:	1650 kg	1690 kg	1770 kg	NA
Trunk capacity:	265 dm³			
PERFORMANCE				
Top speed:	228 kph	240 kph	250 kph	250 kph
Acceleration from 0 to 100 kph:	9.3 sec	8.4 sec	6.2 sec	NA
Km from standing start:	30.1 sec	28.8 sec	25.8 sec	NA
Consumption 90/120/Urban C. (l/100 km):	8.5/10.3/15.9	8.8/10.4/16.2	10.1/12/16.6	NA
Specific power (HP/l):	64.1	78	65.5	68.1
Weight to power ratio (kg/HP):	8.68	7.31	5.42	NA

NA = at the publication date (31/3/92) this datum is not available.

S - JS 9888

The Mercedes SL, slim, clean-lined and perfectly balanced, is not only one of the most successful examples of styling in recent years, but represents a convergence of technology and safety which it is uncommon to find in a car. The body lines, modern yet at the same time conservative, are a harmonious expression of compact elegance which it will be difficult to match.

The SL is not a model which should be judged only for its looks, although there is no doubt that they are delightful. Its overall technological content puts this roadster right in front as far as comfort, safety and driving reliability are concerned.

The 300 SL-24, with the 24-valve 3-litre engine, is perhaps the most balanced, in the context of high class convertibles. The engine has an output of 231 HP at 6400 rpm. It runs regularly and silently, and power delivery is quite smooth. However, the engine lacks a little vivacity at low revs, although it is extremely elastic.

It is a typical multivalve engine, a bit lazy lower down, although it accelerates from 0-100 kph in 8.4 seconds, and is intensely responsive at the top end.

This is not so much due to the maximum torque rating, which is not particularly high in relation to displacement although 27.7 kgm is a very respectable figure, as to the fact that it is achieved at 4600 rpm.

As far as speed is concerned, performance is good: the hard-top version has a top speed of 240 kph.

Three gearboxes are on offer: 2 manual 5-speed transmissions, and a 4-speed automatic.

Of the first two I would advise the one with the closer ratios, which is better suited to this engine.

The automatic has three settings (economic, sports, manual). The first of these settings selects the gears at lower engine speeds, the second is more suited to a sporty use of the car and in the third setting the gears become manual, although not in the real sense of the word. Mercedes' automatic gearboxes are still too attached to the traditional systems.

A car lives in the landscape and not in photographic studios. It is in the landscape that the qualities of its shape, and of course of its mechanicals, are confirmed. The top speeds of the three versions available all round the world vary from 223 to 250 kph.

There are other, considerably more advanced, systems such as the Porsche Tiptronic which provides a real manual alternative and uses sensors in automatic mode to detect sporty driving, and hold the gear, overriding release.

On the road the 300 SL-24 is pleasant to drive and above all is safe at all times. It even manages to be entertaining, although it is not a car suited to sporty driving. Not because it gets difficult to control, on the contrary, as far as this aspect is concerned it is almost too easy, but because its response is not as fast as it should be.

Too much pedal on tight bends reveals an excessive tendency to understeer which is not much fun for a sporty driver, and in order to compensate this tendency with power oversteer the pedal has first to be sharply released and then decisively floored. This is a manoeuvre which can only be carried out near maximum torque, otherwise the understeer only increases.

However, this is not the right way to judge the 300 SL. One should not forget that this is not a sports car in the most extreme sense of the word, but a magnificently elegant cabriolet capable of providing both speed and pleasure as long as it is driven with skill. If this is born in mind the car will not be a disappointment.

Steering is precise and at the beginning may even seem a little rapid in responding to directional commands, but that is how it

In its open version the car's performance and its fuel consumption figures are both slightly penalised. The most efficient aerodynamic configuration is with the hard-top, but with the hood up too performance was close to optimum.

After the road, test the SL at rest in a pleasant environment...

should be. Perhaps the servo system does lighten it a little too much: at top speeds I should prefer it to be a little heavier, it is easy to narrow the turn-in angle too far.

However, this is another problem which only emerges when the car is driven like a sports car.

The brakes are powerful and perfectly in line with the car's performance. The ABS, standard fitting, is excellent, and underlines the contribution of anti locking brakes in terms of safety.

With the 500 SL we enter the realm of very high power and high performance, presented however in line with Mercedes philosophy, which is prepared to sacrifice fun on the driver's behalf in order not to transcend the limits of safety.

The engine is a 4 valves per cylinder, 5-litre V8, with an output of 326 HP at 5500 rpm, maximum torque of 45.9 kgm at 4000 rpm.

This is the best there is as far as smooth running and progressive power delivery goes, although in this case the best is held back until the needle goes over 4000 rpm.

Powerful enough not to mourn the lack of thrust at low engine speeds, it goes from 0-100 kph in a little over 7.0, stopping at the artificial top speed of 250 kph.

The 500 SL is only available with the 4-speed automatic, and so the comments I made on the 300 SL-24 also apply here, only more so.

To make driving easier for their clients Mercedes have fitted ASR traction control on the 500 SL, and it is an optional on the 300 SL. The system controls traction on each wheel in ratio to grip.

This takes away the fun for sporty drivers, but undoubtedly increases active safety, eliminating the danger of power overdrive, a common problem on rear wheel drive cars.

This means that behaviour becomes neutral even if there is the slightest oversteer when turning into tight bends. The adaptive suspensions (ADS) are greatly to be appreciated. Automatically and in real time the system gradually stiffens the shock absorbers in relation to speed, smoothing out bumps caused by load transfer on rough surfaces and winding roads.

Steering is precise and responsive, but in this case too, perhaps even more so than on the 300 SL, it is too light at high speed to be fully satisfying.

The brakes, here again with standard ABS, draw up the car's considerable weight in good time, and the homogeneity of behaviour on both axles is worthy of note.

S-JW 5113

Automobilia wishes to thank Mercedes-Benz AG of Stuttgart and Mercedes-Benz Italia for supplying material and for their assistance in producing this book.